Tawanda Prince

(((Echoes)))
Of My Mind
Now, Then and Forever

Tawanda Prince

(((Echoes))) of My Mind

(((Echoes)))
Then, Now and Forever

Tawanda Prince

Rosie Lane
PUBLISHING

Tawanda Prince

Printed in the United States of America
25 24 23 22 21   987654321

Publisher: Rosie Lane Publishing *rosielanepublishing@gmail.com*
Author's website: *www.tawandaprince.com*
coachtawandaprince@gmail.com

ISBN: 978-0-578-87226-1
Library of Congress registration: TXu-2-260-826
Book design: Tawanda Prince
Cover design: Kendall King- *kkproductions.biz*
Back cover photo: A. Danielle Photography-
adaniellephotography.com
Editor: Wendy Stevens

(((Echoes))) of My Mind

DEDICATION

This book is dedicated to the sweet memory of my friend Angela Parker.

ANGELA-OUR ANGEL

The Lord has called you back
To your rightful place
From heaven you came
And to heaven you have returned
Your time here with us was just a short while
But you will forever remain in our hearts
Shining brightly and reflecting
The precious love of the Father
Helping to illuminate the path to goodness
We shall miss you more
Than mere words can convey
Because you meant more to us
Than mere words could ever say
And as you rejoice around the throne
We will always remember how your light
Touched our hearts and changed our lives
Forever...

A-Always there when needed
N-Never giving up, never-ending faith
G-Generous heart and Godly spirit
E-Extra special friend to all
L-Loving and leading like Jesus
A-Angel on earth; now in heaven

Tawanda Prince

ACKNOWLEDGEMENTS

As always, I first thank God for my health, strength, gifts and talents. Thank you God for choosing me to bear these gifts and trusting me to carry out my assignment.

Thanks to my ever-loving mom, Rosalind Brathwaite, who has always been my biggest cheerleader. Thanks for all of the love and support. As I looked back on my earlier works, I never would have made it without your "typing" skills.

Daddy, Adolphus Brathwaite, remembering you always with love and sweet memories that warm my heart each day. I have honored you in verse in this book.

Javon and Sarah, I'm so proud as I watch your life stories unfold and you become the beautiful spirits that God promised me you would be. The journey continues...

To my creativity stomping grounds, C.I.P.H.E.R. Tuesdays, Acoustic Thursdays, 25 Mics, Poets for Dinner, The Venue, #1 Space, Downing–Gross Cultural Arts Center, thanks for the space to be me.

"Wen-do"...Tyliesha says, "Thanks again!"

Kendall, thanks for always bringing the creative edge, as only you can!

To my "tribe"; thanks for the good vibes. More "verses and vibes" to come.

Table of Contents

(((Echoes))) of My Mind

(((Echoes))) of My Mind

MY DISCOVERY...

During 2020, the world found itself in unchartered territory. We were all locked inside. We were inside our houses, isolated, alienated and separated from one another. We were forced to work from home, eat meals at home, entertain ourselves at home and reclaim our lives at home. Well, I discovered hidden treasures, while at home. Yes! Much to my surprise, I found my original poetry writings, including the first piece I ever wrote in the early 1970's. Wow! What a treasure indeed.

I found a journal, poems and even stories that I had written. It was amazing to see how deep my thoughts were during my teenage years and early twenties. *(Note to parents: listen for what your kids are not saying)* The journal that I found was titled "Seasons of Myself." This is important to note, as it is the title of my second poetry book. I had always declared that when I grew up I would write a poetry book and title it "Seasons of Myself." I kept my promise, but what was I to do with this treasure of the original writings that I had now discovered?

As I took a deep dive into my "treasures," I heard an (((echo))). The dictionary definition of an echo *is to be reminiscent of or have shared characteristics of: resound with or to reflect back; a close parallel or repetition of an idea, feeling, style or event.* As I read my original works, I recognized that, in many ways, my current work is an echo; reverberating thought patterns. There is truly a resounding echo on the journey from "then" to "now"; indeed *a close parallel or repetition of my ideas, feelings and style*.

It has been said, "The more things change, the more they remain the same." While exploring my treasure, I was reminded that seasons happen over and over again and the

9

echoes of my mind resound through my words. My words have always expressed deep emotions of joy, sorrow, hope, love, friendship, intimacy, regret, wonder, God, light, darkness, wants and needs. I have always understood that at the core of humanity is the basic need to be loved, heard, understood and accepted. The heart contains truths that never change with time. Forever is written one word at a time and collectively those words are timeless treasures.

(((Echoes))) contains carefully selected pieces of poetry that I consider timeless. These timeless pieces are great because they capture the evolution of thought and show my development as a writer, all while preserving my perspective on the issues of life. This is a collection of new reflections, personal favorite archives and reader's best choices. It is also noteworthy to mention that the pieces in this book are not all written from personal experiences, but rather thoughts and perspectives from my observations in life. "WE" (wisdom and experience) has guided me along the path to deeper understanding of the truths revealed to me at an early age. I was so clearly wise beyond my years, however, my recent pieces "echo" what I have always somehow understood and creatively expressed. (((Echoes))) is proof that the more things change, the more they remain the same.
These are the echoes of my mind from then, now and forever...

(((ECHOES))) OF NOW

So, this is me having my say, unapologetically. I'm allowing my emotions to be transparent and to bleed onto these pages. Using nouns, verbs and other words to freestyle and flow in whatever direction I choose. Exposing my thoughts that are sometimes righteous, sometimes contentious and yet at other times, precious. Over the years, my words have been evolving and transforming, but never forsaking truth, (as I see it, of course).

These poems speak to the complexities of life and love; shedding light, shedding tears and shedding fears. I am exposing raw emotions that break through the silence and echo sounds of my soul from the past. As an echo is *a close parallel or repletion of an idea, feeling, style or event*, these poems are (((echoes))).

Echoes of love
Echoes of hope
Echoes of passion
Echoes of grief
Echoes of grace
Echoes of despair
Echoes of faith
Echoes of spirit
Echoes of joy
Echoes of peace
Echoes of me
Echoes of NOW!

Tawanda Prince

THE GREAT GATHERING

Behold, now is the time
Of the great gathering
The collection of souls
Passing through shades of night
For a swift return to the light

A tragedy for most it may seem
Leaving loved ones
To return to Love
The Gardener gathering flowers
From amongst the weeds
Flowers that bloomed
From seeds of fear
Cries ring out in travail
For mercy and grace
But none can cease the great gathering

That which has manifested
As devices of evil
Are only put to good use
In the Gardener's hands
Pruning and tilling
Weeding and killing
Dark veils of fear and sadness
Crushing seeds of hope
For better days ahead
Joy trampled underfoot
In the rush of the great gathering
Unforeseen by most
But only known to some

(((Echoes))) of My Mind

Tawanda Prince

Travelers in the great gathering
Crossing over to the other side of divine
Separation, devastation, indignation
Meditation, filtration, aeration
Tribulation and refertilization
Filling up the holes
Where love used to grow

Only uncertainty is for certain
And the rearrangement
Of all things sure
Weeds parched, dried and shriveled
Draped in shrouds of confusion
Longing to be watered by the blood

Flowers gathered together
Sipping new wine in fields of light
Rejoicing in the great gathering
Where the last are first
And the first are waiting
To be the Gardner's choice

The great gathering
Of sinners and saints
Leaving behind those looking
For a ray of hope
Body and soul
Hungering and thirsting
Longing for reversing
Needing blessings, not cursing
A path of traversing
But left behind
Seeds waiting to germinate

(((Echoes))) of My Mind

Tawanda Prince

And a chance to recreate
That which was destroyed

As the rain falls on the just and the unjust
Behold, now is the time of
The great gathering
Sweeping through the field
This is only the precursor
To what is yet to come
The dividing of the
Chaff from the wheat
Misconstrued as defeat
But patterns always repeat

And new life will spring forth
Beyond the great gathering
Seeds will germinate
And life will emerge from the shadows
The soil has been turned
The former blooms have been burned
And wings have been earned
For freedom that was yearned
And lessons have been learned
All because of the great gathering

(((Echoes))) of My Mind

Tawanda Prince

THIS IS US

God has already written our love story
In the annals of time
History giving birth
To dreams of our love divine
Unable to be defined
By finite lines
Infinitely intertwined
A vision of sweet love
Undetectable to the naked eye
But only by the sacred eye

Our forevers touching each other
And then beyond
Beyond the veil of past mistakes
And wonderings and wanderings
More than love at first sight
But rather at first light
Your soul is bright
A perfect fit for my puzzled heart
I see me in you
And you in me
And you and me
Intertwined perfectly
As we were meant to be
And what we shall see
And what we shall be
Is undetected by the naked eye
But guided by the "son" in the sky
And hidden in the annals of time
A love divine
Two souls intertwined

(((Echoes))) of My Mind

Tawanda Prince

Soul food for my spirit and mind
Now together lost and found
Predestined and bound
Letting love echo and resound
With two voices, one sound
So deep so profound

So right, so right
No longer afraid of things
That go bump in the night
Feet dancing to music
Only heard with a lover's ear
Perfect harmony
Unable to be detected
By the naked eye
Hidden in the annals of time
His girl, her guy
Reflected in the mirror of time
I can completely be myself
Completely wrapped in yourself
Igniting one flame
With the glow of eternity
You opened the door of my heart
To find love again
To try again
To fly above again
The answer to whispered questions to God

Love is an enchanting energy exchange
The rhythm of vibrations unexplained
The satisfaction of a heart reclaimed
Awakened to the sound
Of your heart's calling

(((Echoes))) of My Mind

Tawanda Prince

Defenseless against falling
I've been waiting for you to find me
And for us to discover "we"
An open door for our hearts to explore
A song, a lark and so much more
Where melodies collide
Of two hearts intertwined
Long ago written in the annals of time
Beautiful love, sweet love
Love beautiful, complete love
This is us

Tawanda Prince

RED, WHITE AND BLUE

Red, white and oh so blue
But black lives don't matter to you
Blood flowing, death rising
Mothers crying, black men dying
Abuse of power choking out life
Standing on the wrong side of the blue divide
Where do we draw the line
Why is living while black considered a crime
Forced to surrender the privilege to breathe
In a land where freedom has never been free

Red, white and oh so blue
Hatred and fear overtake you
While poverty is rising, bullets flying
Oppression, depression and voter suppression
Truth unidentified
And justice still denied
Flag waving, hatred raging
Choke holds, neck holds
Replace lynchings of old
And the good old boys use guns for toys
In the killing sport no one wins
Humanity needs humanizing again

Red, white and oh so blue
What does America need to do
Body count rising with unrest in the streets
Real time target practice from those not in sheets
Fists to cuffs, knees to necks
Black to blue, life to death
There is no respect

(((Echoes))) of My Mind

Tawanda Prince

When they go low and we go high
How many people have to die
As we all ask the question why
A nation waiting to be great again
Spills the blood of the innocent

Red, white and oh so blue
Does justice for all include me and you
Life, liberty and the pursuit to breathe
In spite of what others believe
As injustice causes our hearts to grieve
And they wonder why we take the knee
Oh say can you see the real tragedy
The privilege of some is a real travesty
All blood is red and our hearts are blue
Because white is right
And black lives have no value

Red, white and oh so blue
There is no way to escape the truth
Trouble runs deep in our nations veins
Unable to erase the history of pain
Despair destroys dreams
As fear reigns supreme
Pleading, kneeling, marching, feeling
Hopeless, helpless, desperate and separate
Eyes open, hearts wired shut
While others drink from the righteous cup
Tear gas is laughing gas to some
Yet while the masses are overcome
Systems, systematic and systemic
Racism and hatred are the real pandemic
All of the injustice is making us sick

(((Echoes))) of My Mind

Tawanda Prince

Emit Till, Rodney King and Philando Castile
Victims of supremacy from slavery until
Majority rules, people are cruel
Laws and policies are dual
Us against them, them against us
Makes me wanna holler 'cause there's no trust
Oh say can't you see that it's true
America is red, white and oh so blue

Tawanda Prince

LET ME BE

Let me be…
Your warm place
Your safe space
Your sugar and spice
Your partner for life

Your set it off in the streets
Your honey bee in the sheets
Your private dancer
Your stone romancer

The hand to your glove
Your everlasting love
Your joy giver
Your sparkle and glitter

Your partner in crime
Your strength when you're tired
Your calm in the storm
Your soft, sweet and warm

Your no holds barred
Your big joker card
Your stop drop and roll
Your key to your soul

Your ace in the hole
Your swing from the pole
Your half to your whole
Your heat when you're cold

(((Echoes))) of My Mind

Tawanda Prince

Your sounding board
Your melodic chord
Your cook with the dish
Your fantasy wish

Your leave and cleave
Your reason to breathe
Your trick and your treat
Your sticky and sweet

Your girl that is pretty
Your sexy in the city
Your art like Picasso
Your wild thing like Lizzo

Your queen of your tribe
Your verse and your vibe
Your peace and serenity
Your here to eternity

(((Echoes))) of My Mind

Tawanda Prince

PEARLS

Your pearls are not welcome here
Because pearls of wisdom have taught me
You can't put a price on love
But if diamonds are a girl's best friend
And I am worthy of only the best
Pearls simply will not due if love is true

No, you can't put a price on love
And you can't save time in a bottle
And if there were really a magic Jeanie
Would you appear when the smoke disappears
Would your scent linger in the air

Your pearls are not welcome here
They are like snake eyes watching
To see how to devour my heart
A trap of beautiful pearls
So tempting to girls
Who are searching for the real thing

Fake, fakers and faked out
By counterfeit jewels but not like
Real pearls cultivated in the depths of the earth
Smoothed by pressure to be the best
Yet, crushed by too much pressure
Unable to withstand like diamonds
Deceptively beautiful to the naked eye
The eye without vision for truth
The eye that searches for meaning and acceptance
The eye that is asleep though wide open

23

(((Echoes))) of My Mind

Tawanda Prince

Your pearls are not welcome here
Your offering of a whore's ransom
For a job well done
Stringing my feelings along
Like a strand of dirty pearls
Not a thing of beauty
Worthy of so much more

Keep your pearls
Keep your gifts
Keep your rose petals and thorns
Keep your lies
Keep your games
Your pearls are not welcome here

Tawanda Prince

IT IS WHAT IT IS

Haters gonna hate
Healers gonna heal
Waiters gonna wait
Stealers gonnna steal

Dreamers gonna dream
Seers goona see
Doers gonna do
Cheaters gonna cheat

Leapers gonna leap
Diggers gonna dig
Players gonna play
Givers gonna give

Takers gonna take
Talkers gonna talk
Makers gonna make
Walkers gonna walk

Marchers gonna march
Lovers gonna love
Launchers gonna launch
Shovers gonna shove

Movers gonna move
Shakers gonna shake
Sleepers gonna sleep
Fakers gonna fake

Carers gonna care

(((Echoes))) of My Mind

Tawanda Prince

Bearers gonna bear
Tearers gonna tear
Sharers gonna share

Foolers gonna fool
Teachers gonna teach
Pray-ers gonna pray
Preachers gonna preach

Winners gonna win
Losers gonna lose
Leaders gonna lead
Choosers gonna choose

Savers gonna save
Spenders gonna spend
Lenders gonna lend
Benders gonna bend

Breathers gonna breathe
Snoozers gonna snooze
Leavers gonna leave
Boozers gonna booze

Risers gonna rise
Criers gonna cry
Try-ers gonna try
Flyers gonna fly

People are who they are
Not what we want them to be
So it is what it is
Truth is in the mirror to see

(((Echoes))) of My Mind

Tawanda Prince

SUN TIME

Sunset wrap your arms around me
Stroke my hair with your rays
Ease the melancholy of the day
Give my thoughts a safe place to settle
Sweet, sweet sorrow at your descending
The glory of the day fading
Yellows, oranges and the blues
Blending into darkness
Giving way to the moon and the stars

Sunrise greets me with a morning kiss
Warm and promising on my face
Awaking my spirit with the dawning
Yellows and oranges welcome the blues
Bursts of light giving way to light
Moon just a memory of what will soon come
Sun embracing me in any season
Arriving without calling
Always welcomed without being summoned

Sunrise gives way to sunset
Divinely dancing and exchanging glances
Yellow dancing with orange, singing the blues
Twins rising and falling
And yet again, rising and falling
Time can never erase your face
Darkness can never harness your light
Sunrise, sunset, hello and goodbye
A mystery divinely etched in eternity

(((Echoes))) of My Mind

Tawanda Prince

I MET A BOY

I met a boy from Brooklyn
And he loved me like
Bagels, cheesecake and Coney Island
Sometimes salty, sometimes sweet
Stole my heart just like a thief
But it didn't last...

I met a boy from DC
And he loved me like
Crab cakes, go-go and mumbo sauce
He stretched my heart from "Soufeast" to Northwest
Promised me memorials and monuments
But it didn't last...

I met a boy from Jersey
And he loved me like
Cannolis, hoagies and salt water taffy
Made my heart laugh, but cry even more
Our thing was steamy like the Jersey shore
But it didn't last...

I met a boy from L.A.
He loved me like
Sushi, avocado toast and Disneyland
We shared sunsets and held hands
As we ran barefoot in the sand
But it didn't last...

I met a boy from the Bronx
He loved me like
Bodegas, White Castle and City Island

28

(((Echoes))) of My Mind

Tawanda Prince

He made my heart bounce, roll and skate
Promised me the world out on the fire escape
But it didn't last...

I met a boy from Virginia
He loved me like
Boiled peanuts, blue crabs and country ham
He said Virginia is for lovers
Then he kept me under cover
But it didn't last...

I met a boy from Philly
He loved me like
Cheesesteaks, soft pretzels and neo-soul
He promised me more than brotherly love
Said he would place no other girl above
But it didn't last...

I met a boy from Baltimore
And he loved me like
Sno-balls, chicken boxes and Billie Holiday
Promised to spice it up all the way
Like seafood with Old Bay
But it didn't last...

I met a boy from the Caribbean
And he loved me like
Beef patties, ganga and trade winds
Said he would make me his queen
If I let him slip in between
But it didn't last...

(((Echoes))) of My Mind

Tawanda Prince

I met a man from Galilee
And He loved me like
He would die for me
His word says He went to Calvary
To give me the gift of eternity
His love is everlasting!

Tawanda Prince

IT'S A GIRL!

It's A Girl!
A long awaited blessing
A dream fulfilled
Born with the name of a princess
But not with riches or privilege
But with purpose

Strong
A lioness at heart
Yet tenderhearted
And taking charge is her gift to the world
Walking boldly in the light of the king
As the princess she was born to be

Princess
The seed of a Prince
She was kissed with royalty
Not with rubies or diamonds
But with pearls of wisdom beyond her years
From the moment of her birth

Beautiful
She owns the crown that she wears
The world makes room for her
As she boldly walks in her royal birthright
But not with riches or privilege
But with purpose

My daughter
A long awaited promise
A jewel in my own crown
Always at the center of my heart
My pride and joy
My special gift from God

(((Echoes))) of My Mind

WELCOME HOME

My heart had been held captive
By your absence
Tears for the vacant occupancy
Unable to touch your face
Or hold your hand
Longing to hear the joy in your voice
Replacing loneliness and pain
Decisions made for personal gain
Pressing down on those who remained
Faithful with love and support

Joy of your chance to return
Only overshadowed by God's choice
To gift us with you
And bringing you home
For that first Thanksgiving together

A mother's heart stretched wide open
Across the foreign seas
To unknown lands
But love knows no bounds
And still my heart beat with yours
Longing for the day
To hold your face in my hands again
And tell you I love you

Welcome home means
You are where you always belong
Where you will always have a seat at the table
Where silence means I love you

Tawanda Prince

Just as a hug means
I'm with you always

On this Thanksgiving
We give thanks for your return
Your presence is welcome
As it has long been longed for
And although through the years
You may make a home
Anywhere else in this world
You will always have a seat at the table
And this will always be
Home sweet home

Tawanda Prince

I TOOK A CHANCE

I took a chance on love
And for a minute
I was riding high
Blinded by the dreams locked away
In a heart long forgotten

I took a chance on love
But love deceived and betrayed me
Leaving me with only me
Scars of a wounded heart
And sweet memories of you

I took a chance on love
I leaped before I looked
I loved before I learned
I fell before I could flee
I committed without being careful

I took a chance on love
But love played a dirty trick on me
Played catch-me-if-you can
And hide-and-go-seek
But in the end nobody wins

I took a chance on love
And joyfully played the fool
Hoping this time it would be different
This time love would be true
Only to be hurt by you

(((Echoes))) of My Mind

Tawanda Prince

I took a chance on love
And the chance I took
Proved to only be a fool's folly
Leading down a tear stained path
To cross the bridge of no return

I took a chance on love
But love turned its back on me
Had me handcuffed
To an impossible dream that would never be
A sweet encounter but not an eternity

I took a chance on love
But instead I found truth
The heart is deceptive even unto itself
The tongue spins lies that weave heartache
The eyes cast shadows on reality

I took a chance on love
Who was an unfair opponent
A master of deception
A master of wit and wonder
That always makes you wonder, what if...

And I would take a chance on love again
Because there is a chance that next time
Love will last

Tawanda Prince

WHEN A LOVE HAS DIED

What do you do when a love has died
And you can't count how many tears you've cried
You wonder what and even sometimes why
You can't understand why he wouldn't try

What do you do when a love has died
But neither one wants to say goodbye
Now he can't even look you in the eye
You know it is just a matter of time

What do you do when a love has died
The heart turned left, instead of right
A giant hole where he used to lie
Nothing but ashes where love once thrived

What do you do when a love has died
Words escape because truth is denied
And passion and love are in short supply
Kisses replaced with silent cries

What do you do when a love has died
You now turn away from what was inside
Welcome mat replaced with
A "No Trespassing" sign

What do you do when a love has died
And nobody seems to even care why
Sweet memories remain of all the good times
But just wasn't enough for love to survive

(((Echoes))) of My Mind

Tawanda Prince

What do you do when a love has died
What was so strong, now weakness abides
You know there is no other remedy to try
So you just cry and cry and say goodbye

Tawanda Prince

EXTREME CHRISTMAS MAKEOVER

Well what do you know it's that time of year
Everyone is looking for Santa and reindeer
But the word on the street and on everyone's lips
An extreme Christmas makeover is the perfect gift

No, this year Santa will not fly in on a sleigh
Instead we'll have Jesus leading the way
The old Christmas tree will need to be tossed
This year Christmas means Christ on the cross
No more stockings hung by the chimney with care
Because our hard hearts are in need of repair
No eggnog or pudding, no cookies to bake
This year we'll get rid of the Christmas that's fake
The wreath on the door won't be seen again
Cause he wore a crown on his head for our sins
No Dasher, no Dancer, no Rudolph's red nose
This Christmas God's glory is all that will show

No carolers will come singing fa la la la la
Instead we should all look to follow the star
No more decking the halls with ivy and holly
Start hanging up things that are sacred and holy
No wagons, no dollies, no bright shining toys
Christmas should celebrate the birth of one boy
No candy canes, sugar plums and no gingerbread
Christ brings new life to that which was dead
No gift cards, no lay-away, no returns to be made
Christ came to earth so your debt would be paid
God is making a list and checking it twice
Is your name written down in the lamb's book of life

(((Echoes))) of My Mind

Tawanda Prince

This year try a makeover it won't be too hard
You must simply return your heart back to God
So when someone asks you what's first on your list
An extreme Christmas makeover is the perfect gift

Tawanda Prince

YOU GOT ME

You got me sprung
And I haven't even touched you
But in my mind
One day is like forever
And we dance the dance
And you are mine

You got me hooked
And we haven't even kissed
Though in my mind
I've tasted the sweet wine
From your sweet lips
And I'm intoxicated

You got me pressed
And we haven't spent time
Yet in my mind
We have journeyed for miles
Through fields of springtime
And I inhale and exhale

You got me tripping
And we haven't even dreamed together
Yet in my mind
The mystery behind your smile
Is so captivating
And I am captured

You got me cold crushing
And we barely even know each other
But in my mind

(((Echoes))) of My Mind

Tawanda Prince

You are so familiar
Yet still so unknown
And I'm shaken not stirred

You got me, you got me
You got me, you got me
And in my mind
Though I was uninvited
The question remains
Will you let me stay

(((Echoes))) of My Mind

Tawanda Prince

LOST AND FOUND

Are you everything I longed for
What my heart has searched for
Butterflies in my stomach
Can't eat
Can't sleep
Can't wait to see you again

It's been a long time coming
But so worth waiting for
And better than I imagined
Discovering you
Exploring new
Fitting the piece in the puzzle

Wisdom says to take my time
Folly wants to throw caution to the wind
Ready to leap again
To feel
To love
But afraid to trust my foolish heart

The path to love has been a winding road
Before and after paint a different picture
View is cloudy, with a chance of showers
Emotions rain
Feelings reign
I can't stop myself from falling

Tawanda Prince

I hear the dam breaking
I feel the tide rushing
I'm quickly losing my grip
Shaky ground
Turned around
My heart is lost and found

Tawanda Prince

REFLECTIONS

Today I looked in the looking glass
And saw your eyes
As tears seeped from mine
Oh, how I remember
How your eyes gazed upon me
With love and pride and joy
How those eyes cried
When life dealt me sadness
And they missed me after a long absence
Those eyes laughed with me
And sometimes at me
But always with love
Even when you couldn't hide
Your rare disappointment

Those beautiful brown eyes
Outlined with dark blue
A gift from my daddy's dad
The windows to your soul
And so much more
Those eyes have now closed
Shutting out this world
And leaving behind eyes that cry
But always peeping at me
When I gaze in the mirror
And when my eyes cry
From missing you too much
I can always find you there
In my reflection

WITHOUT WORDS
For "Davie-Boy Michener"

"Davie-Boy" without words you changed our world
Without words you taught us to love without limits
Without words you taught us grace
Without words you taught us to live simply
Without words you taught us to seek and find joy
Without words you gave us the gift of silence
Without words you showed us that life is merely lived at
its best untangling a skein of yarn
Without words you showed us that a smile is worth
10,000 hellos
Without words you showed us that unspoken
sentiments are the best ones
Without words you taught us to trust God to meet our
daily needs
Without words you taught us that the best things in life
really are free
Without words you taught us to be free
Without words you taught us to believe
Without words you showed us faith in action
Without words you taught us to love, give and serve
more
Without words you showed us the courage to be a light
in a dark world
Without words you reminded us that our weaknesses
are strengthened through God

Tawanda Prince

Without words you reminded us that our imperfections
are perfect in in the maker's hands
Without words you showed us the truth that divine gifts
come without repentance
Without words you taught us that perfect love casts out
all fear
Without words you made us all stop and smell the
flowers
Without words you reminded us that time is precious
and to cherish every moment
Without words you taught us that love is measured
moment by moment
Without words you taught us what it means to be
AUTASTIC!
Without words you proclaimed the message of peace in
the midst of a storm
Without words you returned to the Creator of heaven
and earth and all things good
Without words you returned to the light from which you
came
Without words you left a trail of broken hearts
Without words we say FAREWELL "DAVIE-BOY"

(((ECHOES))) OF THEN

Is it then; or is it now, or is it every now and then? Thoughts come and go, and come again. The funny thing is, what was then, was once now. The origins of our thoughts are the foundation for our words. Do these words and thoughts shape our lives or do our lives reflect our words and thoughts? Or is it just a cycle that repeats mistake...regret...lesson...growth...blessing? In order to have evolution of thought and elevation of experience, you must start somewhere. That "somewhere" is the starting point that leads to the breaking point or turning point.

These pieces share my view of life from where I stood over several decades. They are about love, life, the black experience and my identity and independence. Some of these poems reflect a perspective gathered by my ear hustling adult conversations and listening to "grown folks" music. After all, in the early 1970's, what could I possibly know about "love" anyway?

These early verses, created from experience, observation or imagination, are the foundation for my poetic journey. Whether fully known or simply understood, these poems demonstrate wisdom far beyond my years. So regardless if "then" reflects "now" or "now" reflects "then" it is all a resounding (((echo))).

Tawanda Prince

MY "THANG"
(1982)

a poem
in my rhythm
and my rhyme
a song
with expressions
of my being
there is no
right or wrong
only feelings
one, two
one, two
this beat is mine
no, no, no
you can't have it
to laugh or cry
at my will
these words
in this style
are mine
sassy, saucy, snappy
step, step
keep in step
with my dance
my "thang"
i command the space
between these lines
can't you see
me soar
this spirit
my spirit
strong enough

(((Echoes))) of My Mind

Tawanda Prince

to raise up
the souls of the dead
dead to my world
that is
and
this poem
this song
this dance
this "thang"
will come to
an end
when I say
it is
Done.

(((Echoes))) of My Mind

Tawanda Prince

LOVE IS A VERY FUNNY GAME
(First written poem-circa early 1970's)

Your lips are like cherries that grow in my heart
Your eyes are like dewdrops, we could never depart
I love you so dearly until it's a shame
Love, love is a very funny game

Love is something you sign in a card
Yet, love is something you hold in your heart
Love has a meaning defined in more than one way
You love them tomorrow, but hate them today
Love can come in a minute and leave in the same
Love, love is a very funny game

Love is a feeling you feel deep inside
Sometimes it makes you happy
Sometimes it makes you cry
I get chills all over when I hear your name
Love, love is a very funny game

So remember me honey
I'll remember you too
Remember that we once had
A love that was true

(((Echoes))) of My Mind

Tawanda Prince

FRAGILE
(1981)

Shell made like glass
So delicate to the touch
Contents clear and visible
But not so easily accessible

Purpose only to protect my soul
Though not the case
My wounds doubly exposed
Myself so transparent

Me packaged by me
And stamped FRAGILE
But which end is up
On the verge of shattering

To be HANDLED WITH CARE
Or not handled at all

(((Echoes))) of My Mind

Tawanda Prince

A BLACK GIRL'S PRAYER
(1977)

Bless the girl whose skin is black
The girl who cries out for respect
The girl who has almighty strength
To face the world with all its threats
The girl whose heart was stepped upon
The girl who loved with none returned
The girl whose eyes have cried all night
Yet in the morning is smiling bright
The girl whose face reflects her pain
The girl who needs her life to change
God, bless the girl whose skin is black

Bless the girl whose skin is black
The girl who wonders who she is
The girl who drowns herself in tears
The girl who died although she lives
The girl who needs someone to give
The girl who lives from day to day
Praying her sorrows were swept away
The girl who sings although she is sad
The girl who smiles yet things are bad
The girl whose life is filled with pain
The girl who springs right back again
God, bless the girl whose skin is black

Bless the girl whose skin is black
Who prays the time will quickly come
When all girls stand together as one
The girl who hopes the day is near
When black girls no longer live in fear

52

(((Echoes))) of My Mind

Tawanda Prince

When we can walk with heads high in the air
No longer judged by skin color and hair
The girl who looks to the future to see
A world where black girls have equality
But while things stay where they are at
God, bless the girl whose skin is black

Tawanda Prince

B-EARTH-DAY
(1982)

Deep, dark, oceans
Warm and sticky
Liquid security blanket
Every inch a utopia
Soothing rhythm kept
By two heartbeats
Precious bond of life from life
Snug, so snug
Protected from the pains of birth
So at home in mother's womb

Unwanted freedom
Inflicted upon you
Abruptly evicted from
Your peaceful dwelling
Rudely awakened to the light
Of another world

First seconds
Not filled with mother's breath
Life
Not protected by mother's womb
Birth blessed
By mother's kiss

(((Echoes))) of My Mind

Tawanda Prince

OUTSIDE
(1982)

Outside.
a mere perimeter existence
can't penetrate
no, no
can't get in

forced to create
one's own world
extraordinary
in its own right
still, so alone

Want nothing more
than to belong
won't conform
can't reform
remain so,
Outside

Tawanda Prince

THE RHYTHM
(1998)

The rhythm
It calls me
The beat
It enthralls me
My hands come together as one

The rhyme
It finds me
The time
It unwinds me
My feet respond to the call

S-Y-N-C-O-P-A-T-I-O-N
It moves me
The downbeat
It grooves me
The rhythm, it has no end

The high-hat
Will cling
The cymbals
They ring
The sound it beckons me come

Paradiddles
They drive me
Flamadiddles
They guide me
The rhythm, the rhythm gives me life

(((Echoes))) of My Mind

Tawanda Prince

The rhythm
It makes me
The beat
It takes me
As my feet move to the cadence call

(((Echoes))) of My Mind

Tawanda Prince

LOVE IS
(1977)

Love is desire that's deep down inside
Love is something that you cannot hide
Love is a feeling that will never decay
Love is something that's here to stay
Love is something in both young and old
Love is not materialistic, but as good as gold

Love is the thing that can make mountains move
Love is something that will never lose
Love is a feeling that you can't explain
Love is the thing that will overcome pain
Love is the thing on which the world revolves
Love is the answer to a problem unsolved

Love is a feeling you feel deep inside
Love is the magic that can hush a baby's cry
Love is a feeling we sometimes regret
Love is a feeling we never forget
Love is an emotion and there is no doubt
Love is the one thing we can't live without

(((Echoes))) of My Mind

Tawanda Prince

TAN, BUT NOT BROWN
(A Light Skinned Girls Lament)
(1983)

And they say
I don't have
Enough soul
Not black enough,
Just tan
And my beautiful black sisters
Don't understand
What I have to bear

Light and airy
Like those fairytale princesses
Not a chance to be real
Not a chance to be
Black
Like me

Set me up high
Above the rest
Adorned with a
Semi-golden crown
Who needs that anyway
Labelled, but not loved
They all have their
Names for me
Sometimes even
Black b***h
If I'm lucky
At least they said
BLACK!

59

(((Echoes))) of My Mind

Tawanda Prince

Hey sister, sistah!
This is me
Weren't we both
Birthed at the Nile
Foretold and loved by
Egyptian queens and kings
And now you turn
Your backs on me
And say I'm not
Black enough
I don't have enough soul
Shut me out
Cause I'm
Tan, but not BROWN

Tawanda Prince

A LAYING ON OF HANDS
(2001)

A laying on of hands
Healing hands
Feeling hands
Loving hands
Serving hands
Reaching hands
Preaching hands
Praying hands
Preparing hands
Purifying hands
Sanctifying hands
Exploring hands
Restoring hands
Mending hands
Tending hands
Understanding hands
Commanding hands
Encouraging hands
Nurturing hands
Searching hands
Giving hands
Living hands
Forgiving hands
Inspiring hands
Blessing hands
Confessing hands
De-stressing hands
Planning hands
Expanding hands
God's hands
Your hands

(((Echoes))) of My Mind

Tawanda Prince

LADIES OF LITERATURE
(1982)

To dream, to try
To be like those
Ladies of literature
Queens of distinction
Tellers of truth
More than fluent
But affluent with
Passion and deep compassion
For words and thoughts
Assigning meaning to feelings
And resurrecting feelings from nothing

Ladies of literature
Queens of language like
Maya, Ntozake, Nicki and Toni
All creatures of creation
Maidens of lyrical magic
Using words as weapons
Or to wonderfully woo you

Full of color and life
Spirit and glory of the morning
Daughters of the midnight moon
But never afraid of the dark,
Herself
In the mirror

Fiction and fantasy

(((Echoes))) of My Mind

Tawanda Prince

Folktales and mystery
Prose and poetry
Rhythm and blues in me
And the words
Pirouette on the page
Keeping in step
With the writer's command

At the stroke of the pen
She can make you cry, laugh
Scream and shout
Lie down and play dead
Or shadow dance with dangling participles
Carefully choreographed with commas and such
All while letting her heart bleed on the page

Yes, to dream
To try to be
Like those ladies of literature
Queens of distinction
Tellers of truth
I discovered that
I am
Because they are in me

(((Echoes))) of My Mind

Tawanda Prince

TROUBLE MAN
(For Marvin Gaye)
(1984)

Oh Trouble Man
Sweet lover man
Tormented by inner gloom
Destined to be plagued by doom
Longing for the right one to love
Spirit soaring up above
Crying both inside and out
Trying against the strongest doubts
Consumed and haunted by your fears
Drowned inside your tormented tears
Plagued by demons from your past
Watching dreams fade too fast
Dead before your dying day
Trouble has taken you away
Oh Trouble Man dry your eyes
No blues to sing, no more tears to cry
Trouble Man we all can see
Now your soul's at peace
Your spirit is
FREE...

Tawanda Prince

SHE IS
(1981)

She is compassion
So much more than full woman
The ultimate of beauties
And seems to be all knowing
Most times, my best friend
Sacrificial love extending far beyond
The barriers of life's circumstances

She knows me
Sometimes better than
I know myself
And always strives to make me better
Sharing her light of hope and faith
Always giving, asking for nothing in return
But love and gratitude

Her love is never ending
Even when she suffers great injustices
And she will be there with me
Even after she is gone
She will always be a part of me
She is the gift of love
She is my mother

(((Echoes))) of My Mind

Tawanda Prince

SUMMERTIME
(2000)

Lake Sebago
Fried chicken
Ritz crackers
Green plaid picnic bag

Pink blanket
Pink lemonade
Sand in my shoes
Uncle Charlie

White bathing cap
Corner spot under the tree
Playing cards
Laughter

Wet ponytails
Shovel and pail
No school
Summertime

EXCUSE ME, BUT THAT BELONGS TO ME
(Circa 2000)

Take your hands off of it
Don't touch it, don't you dare
In case you weren't aware
That belongs to me

Don't man handle, or pan handle it
Don't ask to try a sample
It's not yours for the taking
That belongs to me

You had it, you broke it
It hurt 'cause you choked it
Don't pinch it don't poke it
Cause that belongs to me

Don't peak it, don't tweak it
Don't you dare try to sneak it
Don't pick it, don't lick it
Because that belongs to me

Don't smell it, don't taste it
When you had it you wasted it
Don't try to walk away with it
Because that belongs to me

Don't play with it, don't lay with it
When you had it you hated it
No you can't stay with it
Because that belongs to me

(((Echoes))) of My Mind

Tawanda Prince

Don't grease it, don't squeeze it
You didn't know how to please it
Too weak to receive it
'Cause that belongs to me

Don't tease it, don't taunt it
I got it, and I'll flaunt it
Don't put your hands on it
'Cause that belongs to me

So I'll pack it, I'll stack it
I'll fold it and hold it
I'm the one who controls it
Because that belongs to me

(((Echoes))) of My Mind

Tawanda Prince

NIGHT BIRD
(1982)

Night bird come
And take me away
For my lover awaits me
In the dark
Still I am just
A figment of his dreams

Night bird soar
And carry me quick
By the light of the moon
To my lovers bed
For he knows not
If I will come

Night bird hurry
My soul longs to fly
My lover can't wait
The morning comes soon
Deliver me safe
From the heat of the night

(((Echoes))) of My Mind

Tawanda Prince

SWEET BEGINNINGS
(1980)

Time has passed
And the mystery has unfolded
Oh, those sweet beginnings
Filled with the freshness
And tenderness
That only comes with
That first kiss

Two hearts skipping every other beat
And trying to understand
This blissful newness
Did we get lost in each other
Or just lost in ourselves
Now that it's done
Will we forget its beauty and life

Oh so perfect it seems
No substance, just vibrations
No truth, just a heart's imagination
Like a flower
Will we bloom then close up and die
Or will we let our flickering spark
Be a forever burning flame

Each touch and each kiss
An even greater sensation
How perfect and complete it seems
But it's only the beginning

(((Echoes))) of My Mind

(((ECHOES))) OF FOREVER

These pieces are my favorites. They are the ones that strike a little deeper, hit a little harder or make my heart smile. Whether it is the poetic style, the words or the inspiration behind the piece, these have also become crowd favorites. This collection of "greatest hits" echoes loudly the high, low, deep and shallow vibrations of my poetic journey.

Forever, eternal, never ending, into infinity and beyond! These timeless pieces are curated from my two previous poetry collections, **Nouns, Verbs and Other Words** and **Seasons of Myself**. As an echo is *to resound with or to reflect back*, these words are dancing on the page to the beat of my soul and the vibe is good always and FOREVER.

Tawanda Prince

THUNDER KNOCKING
AT MY HEART

That day I stood so unaware
How God would keep me in His care
Thunder came knocking at my heart
It was that day my life fell apart
I stood so still as thunder rolled
I held on tight but lost control
My heart was troubled but still it beat
Until thunder knocked me off my feet

My heart began to tremble and shake
When thunder roared my life was at sake
I had no choice, no turning back
I was having a heart attack
Fear and darkness covered my way
Help me Lord is all I could say
Thunder rolled and death I saw
As good and evil battled a war
Death tried to take me but God said no
This is my servant, she cannot go
I have much work for her to do
The plans I have she must pursue

Thunder rolled three times more
Each time leading me to an open door
To step out on faith, with God to stand
And to follow his anointed plan
When thunder knocked my heart I gave
From death and hell my soul was saved
When thunder knocked I had no choice
But to heed the command of God's voice

72

(((Echoes))) of My Mind

Tawanda Prince

He told me to go out and tell the world
How he healed the heart of a broken girl
After thunder knocked a rainbow came
My life will never be the same
The clouds went away, the sun did shine
Now the promise of new life is mine
Each day is a gift I open to see
What God has in his plan for me
Thunder knocked and I heard the call
To God I give my all and all
There is no doubt, miracles come true
Now my heart is made all brand new

Tawanda Prince

WORD LIQUOR

Just wanna let you know
That words intoxicate me
Nouns, verbs and phrases really fascinate me
Spoken and written down really stimulate me
Do they do the same for you?

Word liquor do you want some
Made for a poet's consumption
Word liquor just sounds so sweet
With a vibe and flow that so unique
Word liquor yes I want that
Sippin' pure facts
Wanna taste that word liquor
You know it's true,
I wanna get drunk off you

Can we just sit down and have a conversation
Just take a sip of some verbal libation
Words that are expressing me
And give me supreme revelation
Do they do the same for you

Write it down so I can sip it slow
Intellectual elixir that makes my rhymes flow
Wanna read and write and say some things
Open up and express my inner feelings
Words I love them wanna let you know
Wanna take my time and sip it slow
Word liquor you know it's true
I wanna get drunk off you
(Inspired by the song Brown Liquor by Marc Evans)

(((Echoes))) of My Mind

Tawanda Prince

THE STRUGGLE IS REAL

We struggle in a world that doesn't accept us
We struggle to make our marks on jobs where they just
suspect us
We struggle in relationships with partners who neglect us
We struggle within families where kinfolk reject us
We struggle to live in neighborhoods where the neighbors
don't respect us
We struggle to escape the history that connects us
We struggle to speak a language that doesn't reflect us
We struggle to be heard in a nation where they don't want to
elect us
We struggle to be led by leaders who misdirect us
We struggle in a system where the laws don't protect us
We struggle to be loved by lovers who infect us
We struggle to be cured by doctors who just inject us
But we struggle toward the end
When God will resurrect us

Tawanda Prince

SACRED

Water is sacred
Wood, sand and trees are sacred
Lightening, rocks and leaves are sacred
Wind is sacred
Snow is sacred
The way the river flows is sacred
The stars and planets in the sky are sacred
The Light, the Light, the Light is sacred

Fire is sacred
Ice is sacred
The origin of everything nice is sacred
Love is sacred
A deer is sacred
Music to my ear is sacred
My soul is sacred
My hole is sacred
And mysteries that unfold are sacred
Freedom is sacred
Peace is sacred
And every part of me is sacred

Sacred is as sacred does
It's what's to come and what once was
My heart beat is sacred
My breath is sacred
Every single footstep is sacred
My soul is sacred
My spirit is sacred
The God who lives in me is sacred
Prayer is sacred

(((Echoes))) of My Mind

Tawanda Prince

Song is sacred
Tears that babies cry are sacred
Space is sacred
The rain is sacred
And even sometimes my pain is sacred

My flow is sacred
My vibe is sacred
My rhythm and my rhyme are sacred
My joy is sacred
The blood is sacred
The power of God's love is sacred
Sacred is the sun that shines
And sacred berries still make wine
A bee is sacred
A bird is sacred
Nouns, verbs and words are sacred

(((Echoes))) of My Mind

Tawanda Prince

TO BE HONEST

To be honest
Though I no longer cry I can't deny
That I love you
I'm no longer chasing rainbows
With dreams of white lace and white picket fences
I can no longer bear your cross
Or satisfy that monkey on your back
You see the light broke through
And darkness is no longer my dwelling place
Once you see, you can't un-see
Once you know, you can't' un-know
So I must go
To a higher place
Where there is no trace of the stench of
Fermented promises, rotting expectations and you
A place where love and truth really are true
A Place where I can find me

The me, that was lost in the fire of desire for you
The me, that existed before the great fall
And before the great wall of deception
The me, that was thirsty
To taste the wine of delusion
The me, that thought that you would love me
And would not be the fool maker
The me that believed with my heart
Not me eyes that saw the truth

Gray hair says I should know better than to trust a thief
Who knocks on the door in the middle of the night
That it is not alright to borrow or lend a cup of sugar

(((Echoes))) of My Mind

Tawanda Prince

To an unworthy stranger
And as truth is stranger than fiction
I let this depiction of a saint
Baptize me in the murky waters of feel good

And covered with dirt
I emerged with the hurt and broken pieces
Of what used to be my heart
Scales falling from my eyes
As I realized you couldn't save me
Feeling the sting as I breathlessly cling to forever
Forever changed, my crown and pearls rearranged
But I'm still a queen
And it remains to be seen
The beauty that will rise from these ashes

Ashes to ashes and dust to dust
Sadly I must
Add your name to the ex-files
Forever exiled from my precious
With other fakers and heartbreakers
Who will no longer be partakers of my secret sauce
Now I'm the boss
And what I say goes
So you must
Because I can't trust
A liar and a thief
Who stole my belief
In white lace and white picket fences

(((Echoes))) of My Mind

Tawanda Prince

So I'm flushing the toilet
And taking out the trash
Letting go of mistakes from the past
And although I no longer cry
I can't deny that I still love you
But goodbye!

Tawanda Prince

LET THE GOOD TIMES ROLL

Remember the times in days gone by
When we grooved to the sounds of The Jackson Five
Bell bottoms, peace signs and afro hairdos
Freedom was the thing that we fought to pursue
Gladys Knight, The Four Tops and The Temptations
This was a time of living with no limitations
Mood rings, afro picks and a little "bamboo"
Strobe lights, incense and platform shoes
Roller skates, mini-skirts and thigh-high boots
Everybody was busy searching for the truth
But Malcolm, Martin and Medgar died for the cause
Marches and meetings helped to open the doors
Soul train lines, picket signs and riots rang out loud
James Brown taught us to be black and proud
Richard Pryor, Dolomite and Redd Foxx made us smile
Chia pets, bean-bag chairs and phones we had to dial

Then the 80's rolled in with changes in our world
Some wore pink hair while some wore jheri curls
Boy George, Milli Vanilli and Michael was the "Thriller"
Inside and outside of the closet AIDS became a killer
Solid Gold, HBO, Showtime and MTV
Oprah and Arsenio proved that talk ain't cheap
The Cosby Show, A Different World, Prince and Morris Day
"Just Say No" and condoms became the only way

The 90's was a time of change with the 70's all grown up
Bill played the sax, had no sex and didn't inhale the "stuff"
Sister Act, Disappearing Acts, and Ghost was on the screen
Biggie Smalls and Tupac Shakur just up and left the scene

(((Echoes))) of My Mind

Tawanda Prince

Michal Jackson said he did not touch and Magic had HIV
We wore acrylic nails, colored eyes, braids, wigs and weaves
Mike Tyson and O.J. Simpson made headlines more than
twice
Jessie Jackson had a little secret that wasn't very nice

The new millennium in the land of the "Bush" and the pain of
911
Condoleezza and Collin Powell like the Jeffersons had moved
on up
Halle Berry and Denzel Washington made Hollywood history
The Grammys showed Alicia Keys battle India Arie
Ellen came out, Aaliyah flew home and the Columbia blew up
Venus and Serena took home the championship cup
Now the world has changed and changed again with lots of
evidence
The United States of America has a black man President
But marches, meetings and riots still ring out loud
There's Obamacare, iPads, iPods and gays can marry now
Freddie's dead, Trayvon is gone and we can't forget Mike
Brown
Unemployment is up, communities down and homelessness
abounds
American Idol, Empire, Catfish and Orange is the New Black
Drones flew beyond the White House wall perhaps to plan
attack
Whitney's gone, "Housewives" are hot and Scandal is all the
rage
And everyone reveals their lives on their Facebook page
All in all it has been quite a ride that is something to behold
From here and now, time marches on so let the good times
roll

(((Echoes))) of My Mind

Tawanda Prince

HAUNTED HOUSE

Ghosts and goblins
Monsters and ghouls
My house is haunted
Cause I've been a fool
Skeletons in my closet
Bones on my floor
Remnants and fragments
Of a life that is no more

Black cat in the window
Witches brew in the pot
Spooks in the alley
Trying to get what I got
And I gave of myself
When the fire got hot

Jack was no lantern
And the monster didn't mash
The noise that was heard
Was my heart as it crashed
When the mummy came walking
With his crystal balls
My house wasn't ready
Cob webs on my walls
He slipped in beside me
And troubled my head
My house became haunted
When he got in my bed

(((Echoes))) of My Mind

Tawanda Prince

Rats and rattlesnakes
Spiders and worms
Taunting and teasing
Each one took a turn
This vampire was thirsty
For a taste of my blood
Each kiss was more deadly
Each time we made love

Then he just vanished
Before one early dawn
Blood on my carpet
Tombstone on my lawn
Now my house is haunted
There is no doubt
I can't escape it
My secret is out
Skeletons in my closet
Bones on my floor
Remnants and fragments
Of a life that is no more.

Tawanda Prince

FAMILY REUNION

Come one, come all it's that time of year
It's a family reunion and everyone's here
We've come from the north, south, west and east
We all get together to meet, drink and feast
Everyone gathers down at the junction
This family put the fun in dysfunction
They say blessed be the family ties that bind
Sometimes family can make you lose your mind

At the head of the table is Papa Joe
He got another family but nobody knows
There's Cousin Jane so proud and sedity
She got her a woman and they live in the city
And Cousin Suzie so holy and true
Had so many men don't know what to do
Oh there's the twins Johnnie and Jack
One drinks liquor and the other does crack
Cousin Ellie, Cousin Dann and little C.C.
Nobody knows who their daddy be
Blessed be the family ties that bind
Sometimes family can make you lose your mind

Big Mama's in the kitchen cooking up greens
Don't nobody like her because she's so mean
Look over there is sweet uncle Clyde
He's here with his wife, but got a man on the side
Oh look over there it's Uncle Chester
Quiet, hush, hush, he's the child molester
Poor uncle Manny drinks like a fish
It's the only way he can live with Big Sis
Ronnie, Sylvia and butch are in town

(((Echoes))) of My Mind

Tawanda Prince

Gotta make sure we nail everything down
Cousin Mimi is here just as fine as can be
But sorry to say she has 6 personalities
Blessed be the family ties that bind
Sometimes family can make you lose your mind

And Brother Reverend is always preaching'
But he can't seem to keep his wife from creepin'
Lil' Jay Jay comes around flashing big money
But everyone know his paper is funny
And Aunt Louise hasn't spoken for years
She sits in the corner and drowns in her tears
She came with her husband, mean Uncle Nick
He keeps her in check by slinging his fist
Big Cousin Lucy only comes just to be seen
Everyone knows she's a fierce drama queen
There's Cousin Ricky who is fond of the dance
It is easy to see there's a flame in his pants
I just couldn't miss this one chance to see
All the nuts and fruits on our family tree
Blessed be the family ties that bind
Sometimes family can make you lose your mind

(((Echoes))) of My Mind

Tawanda Prince

MY SISTER'S KEEPER

When she is hungry, I feed her
When she is naked, I clothe her
When she is cold, I warm her
When she is hot, I cool her
Am I my sister's keeper?

When she is broken, I mend her
When she is sick, I heal her
When she is crying, I hold her
When she is dying, I revive her
Am I my sister's keeper?

When she is lonely, I comfort her
When she is angry, I calm her
When she is confused, I guide her
When she is misused, I protect her
Am I my sister's keeper?

When she is barren, I birth for her
When she is abandoned, I receive her
When she is burdened, I relieve her
When she is trying, I believe in her
Am I my sister's keeper?

I am my sister's keeper
A charge I can't deny
Her load I bear because I know
In time she'll carry mine
Yes, I am my sister's keeper
Connected through the heart
Every woman is my sister
And nothing can keep us apart
I am my sister's keeper

(((Echoes))) of My Mind

Tawanda Prince

THE MAKING OF A
TRUE WARRIOR

The heart of a true warrior
Is tender yet tough
He beseeches God for guidance and strength
And leans not to his own understanding
With courage he walks boldly into the fire
And he is not defeated by the fiery darts of the adversary

The essence of a true warrior
Is mighty yet meek
He is a conqueror and an overcomer
Though he may slay giants
And climb mountains
He never considers himself more highly than he ought

The spirit of a true warrior
Is resilient yet resigned
To accept his God appointed and anointed assignment
Always restless and ready
To bounce back from any setbacks
Turning stumbling blocks into stepping stones

The valor of a true warrior
Is always seeking to protect and defend the weak
Even if it costs him his own dreams
He is ready for battle
As he keeps watch at the gate
Wearing the full armor of God

The soul of a true warrior
Is playful yet cautious

(((Echoes))) of My Mind

Tawanda Prince

As he carefully orchestrates the dance
Between offensive and defensive maneuvers
He enjoys wielding the sword of the spirit
And lashes offenders with his tongue

A true warrior
Is armed and extremely dangerous
He is always positioned for battle
Courageous in struggle and victorious in warfare
Knowing that he can do all things through Christ who
strengthens him
Are you a true warrior?

Tawanda Prince

RHYTHM APHRODISIAC

And he smelled of incense, exotic oils
And sweet talk
As he passed by
Melodies and cadence
Melodies and cadence

Musical notes dripped from his soul
His gait swayed to rhythms
Of ancient drums and heavenly beats
His horn spoke to me
And called out to ancestors of sacred love
Melodies and cadence
Melodies and cadence

The richness of his ebony skin
Crowned with cascading locks
The perfect back drop for eyes
Deep with visions of
Crescendos and diminuendos
From tribes and generations
Of rhythm and blues
Melodies and cadence
Melodies and cadence

And as he passed by me
Smelling of incense, exotic oils
And sweet talk
Mr. Music man
Made my soul dance
And his midnight black
My rhythm aphrodisiac

90

(((Echoes))) of My Mind

Tawanda Prince

YOU NEVER BOUGHT ME DIAMONDS

You never bought me diamonds
Nor rubies or pearls
Never called me precious
Nor said I was your girl
You never held my hand
To stroll down lover's lane
Never worked to make things better
Never tried to ease my pain

You never bought me diamonds
Nor springtime flowers in bloom
Never called me your honey
Nor asked me to jump the broom
You don't know my favorite color
Nor my favorite kind of tea
You don't know when I started school
Nor finished my degree

You never bought me diamonds
Nor chocolates for me to munch
You never took me to a movie
Or even out to lunch
I have never met your family
And you have not met mine
I don't know the friends you keep
Nor where you spend your time

(((Echoes))) of My Mind

Tawanda Prince

You never bought me diamonds
Nor wrote poems with my name
You never asked what I was feeling
You just simply ran your game
But one day I'll get diamonds
Some flowers, chocolates and all
But for now I'll have to face the fact
It was just a booty call

Tawanda Prince

WEATHER REPORT

Climate changing
Global warming
Hot flashes
Cold shoulder
Artic vortex
Moon rising
Front warming
Clouds forming
Sun setting
Desert storming
Storm warnings
Current raging
Pressure rising
Fire flaming
Spring budding
Sands burning
Leaves falling
Glacier melting
Solstice turning
Water rising
Tide rushing
Jets streaming
Light dawning
Climate changing
Global warming

Tawanda Prince

MR. DISTRACTION

What I thought was a mutual attraction
Was just a pattern of subtraction
Which yielded a negative reaction
So jack you, Mr. Distraction

Of my heart you only wanted a fraction
Which could never bring true satisfaction
Your words never led to real action
So jack you, Mr. Distraction

Your smile seemed to offer benefaction
Empty words were just an abstraction
Merely only a one-sided transaction
So jack you, Mr. Distraction

Pretending you needed real passion
Disappointment was the only extraction
Telling lies was your infraction
So jack you, Mr. Distraction

You wanted benefits without attachment
Desired to play with my contraption
Just a loser's game of entrapment
So jack you, Mr. Distraction

Fabrication leaves a heart in traction
Blocking chances of true love interaction
Fool's gold brings dissatisfaction
So jack you, Mr. Distraction

(((Echoes))) of My Mind

Tawanda Prince

NO MORE

No more crumbs on my table
No more socks on my floor
No more lover who ain't able
No more, no more, no more

No more, "Baby I'm sorry"
No more listening at the door
No more need to sit and worry
No more, no more, no more

No more phone numbers in your pocket
No more hang ups on my phone
No more picture in my locket
No more, no more, no more

No more bills I didn't make
No more keeping score
No more kisses that are fake
No more, no more, no more

No more lies and misunderstandings
No more, "Baby I can't recall"
No more ego that's expanding
No more, no more, no more

No more touches at midnight
No more making love on the floor
No more feeling that feels so right
No more, no more, no more

No more dreams about tomorrow
No more yearning at my core
No more heart that's filled with sorrow
No more, no more, no more

(((Echoes))) of My Mind

Tawanda Prince

CHILD'S PLAY

Sometimes this game of LIFE is like child's play
And I find myself in TROUBLE
It seems to just BOGGLE my mind
That this RING AROUND THE ROSIE
Can leave me playing CHARADES

I often think
Will I just be an OLD MAID
Forever playing RUN CATCH AND KISS
But always falling down the CHUTES AND LADDERS
Never reaching the CANDY LAND

I take my chances using PIXIE STIX
To carefully dissect
The OPERATION of love
And trying to choose the right one
From all the JACKS and BALLS
As I HOP SCOTCH and DODGE BALL
On the MYSTERY DATE, I can't help but to wonder
Will love come NOW AND LATER or
Will I just end up with a MILK DUD instead of a SMARTIE

Will it be another Saturday night
At a table for UNO
Or will I be blessed to
Spend some quality time with a JOLLY RANCHER
Who doesn't think that he has a MONOPOLY
On the MILKY WAY of love
And isn't just some LEMON HEAD trying to steal my
CHOCOLATE KISSES
Which could cause me to

96

(((Echoes))) of My Mind

Tawanda Prince

Use a B-B-BAT as a JAW BREAKER
Or even worse,
Use my BAZOOKA to protect my JUICY FRUIT

I believe you should call a SPADE a spade
But sometimes that leads to WAR and
I might just simply lose my MARBLES and
Use some TWIZZLERS to HANGMAN
Who doesn't even have a CLUE

Oh, how I long for the days
When I was a HOT TOMALE
When IKE & MIKE, and all the MR. POTATO HEADs
Were chasing after my MOUSE TRAP
Just hoping to see my TOOTSIE ROLL
All those CRACKER JACKS wanted to
Mix their BLOW POPs with my MARY JANE
But SORRY, I was very selective with my BIT-O-HONEY
And no matter how many love DARTS they threw at me
I would never CONNECT FOUR
Because that only creates a DOMINO effect
And I couldn't handle the SNICKERS from the crowd

However, there was that one time
When MR. GOODBAR's SLINKY
Got caught up in my LAFFY TAFFY
But that situation was just too much of a TWISTER for me
And it caused too much AGGRAVATION
So GUESS WHO jumped overboard the BATTLESHIP of love
Because my heart was torn to pieces in my CHESS

(((Echoes))) of My Mind

Tawanda Prince

SIMON SAYS that
Good things come to those who wait
So I will have to wait and see
What the MAGIC 8 BALL of love says
Or I could take a chance and SPIN THE BOTTLE
And pray that I don't end up with some
JACK IN THE BOX with ANTS IN THE PANTS
Who just uses my heart for a YO-YO
And leaves me at home playing with my RUBBER DUCKIE

But since there are no guarantees
In this game of LIFE
I can only hope that my PAY DAY will come soon
When I will find my SWEETART
And I won't have to spend the rest of my days
Just playing SOLITAIRE

*(The words in all CAPS may refer to a trade name or trademark of
certain popular childhood games, toys and candy)*

Tawanda Prince

WHILE YOU WERE SLEEPING

While you were sleeping
You held my hand just like when I was a little girl
I felt your strength
Although you were half in another world

While you were sleeping
I sang memories with sweet melodies
And I thought of all the things you taught me
And the special way that you loved me

While you were sleeping
I prayed to God on your behalf
And my heart ached as I watched you
Show your incredible strength as a man

While you were sleeping
I thought of past bike rides
Horseback rides and holidays gone by
And I watched you cry

While you were sleeping
I came face to face with that which
You tried so hard to protect me from
The pain of losing you

While you were sleeping
I watched you fight like the valiant warrior
That you have always been
Even in your hour of weakness

(((Echoes))) of My Mind

Tawanda Prince

While you were sleeping
I longed to hear you speak just one more time
Tell me you love me just one more time
Speak my name just one more time in the silence

While you were sleeping
I wondered if you would wake up
Here or on the other side
And while you were sleeping...I cried

Tawanda Prince

Tawanda Prince's diverse professional profile includes teaching, writing, performing and coaching. She earned a Bachelor of Arts in English from Hunter College and a Master of Arts in Teaching from Bowie State University. She is also a certified Life Breakthrough Coach.

Formerly, Tawanda was an adjunct professor of English at Prince George's County Community College; and an instructor at the University of Maryland. Additionally, she taught high school English, and was nationally recognized in Who's Who Among Americas Teachers in 1996. Currently, she conducts writing workshops and provides book coaching to aspiring authors.

Tawanda Prince is the author of five empowering books, *Wonderful Words of Life, The Good Life, Nouns, Verbs and Other Words, Seasons of Myself* and *Thunder Knocking at My Heart*. She has also written and produced two gospel stage plays, *Timeless: A Soulful Christmas Musical* and *Put A Ring on It!*

Tawanda's creative talents as a poet, singer, songwriter, drummer, radio host and actress have been widely showcased and she has various television, radio, movie and performance credits to add to her list of accomplishments. www.tawandaprince.com